IT'S A MEETING
NOT ROCKET SCIENCE

A MANUAL
FOR MEETINGS

JASON MOORE

© Jason Moore 2016 & 2018. All Rights Reserved.

PB3015

In the last 50 years ordinary men and women have cured countless diseases, saved millions of lives, returned safely from the moon, and removed the pips from fruit.

So why can't we conduct an effective meeting?

I've been looking for an answer to that question for more years than I care to remember. Fortunately, my research shows, it is not beyond the collective awesomeness of humankind to make good use of the talent, energy and wisdom of a small group of well-intended people in a meeting room. Yet, too often meetings are ineffective and unproductive, a place where people get together to chat about what should happen or what needs to happen or what used to happen, before separating into smaller groups, cliques and silos where all the real decisions get made. Alternatively, the group avoids making any decisions at all.

If you doubt my experience, there's lots of fancy research conducted by fancy companies that the fanciest organizations around the world know and trust. In one study, managers said they spend 28 hours a week in meetings and almost a third (31

HOURS
LEADERS WASTE
EVERY MONTH IN MEETINGS

PERCENT
PEOPLE SAY THEY DO
OTHER WORK IN MEETINGS

37 BILLION
ANNUAL US SALARY COST
WASTED IN MEETINGS

hours every month) are a waste of time. And nearly three-quarters of meeting attendees say they do other work in most meetings. That shouldn't surprise us. We've all seen distracted colleagues on phones and laptops. Maybe we're guilty of it ourselves. Based on these numbers, every one-hundred leaders in your organization wastes more than 35,000 hours a year in unproductive, ineffective and unnecessary meetings. A conservative estimate of the cost of all this, just in the United States, is over $37,000,000,000. The global number of wasted hours, effort, energy, financial cost and, let's face it, emotional wellbeing is at least a factor of ten!

In my own research, I've been asking people how satisfied they are with their meetings, on a scale of 1 to 10. At the bottom end of the scale, someone might report they 'hate and dread' their meetings. Whereas others, who score at the top end, tell us they 'love and cherish' them. It won't surprise you that very few people score their meetings as a 10. In fact, as of May 2018, the average level of satisfaction (what I call the Meeting Satisfaction Score) is 5.2. In other words, the vast majority of people tolerate an average meeting rather than enjoying a fantastic one. I think most people don't understand or have forgotten how important meetings are. We've begun to see them as unimportant because, let's be honest, unimportant things are too often done in them. Which is crazy, because a meeting about something, a meeting that inspires and unites and builds trust, with time spent getting things done, being creative, leading, learning and celebrating together is possible and quite simple. It might not feel easy, but that's because we have to overcome deeply ingrained, unproductive and unhelpful habits.

It is worth getting this right.

Meetings are the only time, in most workplaces, when you can get a group of people focused on the same thing at the same time. It is a place to improve things collectively, to switch each other on and to create real organizational value. Meetings are a unique opportunity to use talent, energy and awesomeness to do something that makes a difference.

It's not rocket science.

Everything I've learned about effective, productive and satisfying meetings can be summed up in those four words. So, why are so many meetings unproductive, ineffective and dissatisfying? There are three reasons:

First, most of us don't know what we don't know. We don't attend mandatory training on effective meetings. And there's no manual on the table or instructions on the walls. We learn from doing, and most of us don't know how simple it is to have meetings that we love and cherish.

Second, some people do know but don't care. I meet people all the time who tell me they know how to have 'orgasmic' meetings. When observed, the evidence suggests otherwise. Let's assume then, they know but don't care enough to turn it into action. I've reluctantly concluded that some people don't mind filling their days with unproductive meetings because they have nothing better to do.

Third, we know and care, but are stuck in an unhelpful loop. These are the people who read this book and, despite the simplicity and how easy it can be, they still don't make any changes. It's not because they are bad people, it's because our unhelpful habits regularly undo even our best intentions.

Whichever group you are in, this practical little book can help.

Three promises.

But before we get your meetings more focused, more productive, more satisfying and much shorter (yes, this is for real, your meetings really will get shorter), I am going to make you three promises:

❶ It is simple.

You'll notice this book is quite slim. That's because, as the title says, making meetings significantly better is not rocket science and you do not need to be a rocket scientist or a brain surgeon. There are no complicated concepts, models or processes. You won't need to learn a new language, and you don't need a thousand-page book to make sense of it all.

❷ It is easy.

I am inherently lazy. I look for the easiest way to approach things. I have taken things out of this book because, despite being useful, it made it harder than it needed to be. I want fantastic meetings to be so easy you'll have no excuses. In truth, it's so easy you could fit the whole thing on eight pages (see page 105-113). The other pages are here to help remove as many of the excuses you already have that limit your capacity to be successful and have shorter and better meetings.

❸ It is proven.

I'm not making this stuff up. It is based on years of applied research. I introduced groups to the ideas in the book and watched what happened. Eventually, I just gave an early draft of the book to people and checked in six weeks later.

At that point, eighty-percent of people told me the quality of their meetings had improved. The average Meeting Satisfaction Score for these groups went from under 5 to almost 8. Meetings, seven out of ten people told us, were shorter. Debate became more productive, discussions more punchy and decisions improved.

The core of the work came from two large projects. The first is a global fast moving consumer goods company and the second is an international bank. Combined, these two organisations have almost half a million employees. But all of the concepts have been tested across many different businesses, large and small, in all kinds of industries. They've also appeared in places like the Harvard Business Review and have been studied by lofty academic institutions like Insead Business School in Switzerland.

BEFORE YOU START

I have learned, more often than not, what gets measured gets done. It's a good principle to measure things so we can see our strengths, our areas for development and our progress.

Everything in this book can be measured. I am proposing we start by taking a quick pulse check using the free Better Meeting Assessment, which takes only three minutes and gives you a comprehensive, personalised report. You can complete it on your smartphone, tablet, PC or Mac here:

http://survey.itsameeting.com

Within a few minutes, you'll know which parts of this book are going to help you most.

Two other things will happen when you complete the assessment:

1. Change with your team.

When you get your report, you'll receive a link that can be shared with your team. Pass that unique URL on to your colleagues, and anyone who completes the assessment will receive a personalised report. And, you'll also receive an aggregated report that averages the responses of your colleagues. There's also a TeamTalk session plan to help you discuss how to improve your meetings together.

2. Retest to measure progress.

On the six-week anniversary of your assessment, you'll receive an invitation to retake it. You can then celebrate progress and prioritise your next move.

ONE LAST THING

Forty-two percent of the people who have completed the Better Meeting Assessment say they hope improving their meetings will lead to less of them. The focus of this book is on better, not fewer meetings. Although most people say their meetings are shorter, I can't promise you will have fewer meetings after applying what you learn here, but I do think fewer is better.

Bob Newhart, the American comedian, has a hilarious sketch where he plays a therapist who promises to cure a patient's phobias immediately. He does this by abruptly shouting 'stop it!' as she describes her symptoms (you can watch the sketch here: http://itsameeting.com/stopit/).

I would like you to remember that advice when you are on your way to a meeting you don't need to attend.

Stop it!
Turn around and use that hour for something else. When you catch yourself completing work that does not relate to the meeting you are in, stop it! Either pay attention, help the group be at their best or disinvite yourself.

List your weekly meetings.
Write a list of all the meetings you attend each week. Give each meeting a score between 1 (do not need to be there) and 5 (must attend). Any meetings that score a 1 or 2… stop it! Take them out of your diary. You will be surprised how many meetings fall into this category. Consider carefully the meetings that score a 3 or 4. Is there another way you could approach these meetings? What happens when you are on leave, do these meetings stop? If you cannot entirely justify being there, then you should… stop it!

Better Meeting Habits

●
One big idea.

Organizations are not full of bad people doing bad things. People aren't born lazy, greedy or stupid. We are wired to co-operate, and most people would rather work together than compete. People want to do good work. But even well-intended people don't always know what to do to make things better and often we are unconsciously repeating very unproductive and unhelpful habits. Together, we are going to build some better meeting habits. We will do this by opening our minds to:

●●
Two Simple Roles.

When starting a meeting assign two roles: the **Timekeeper** (manages the time) and the **Submarine Commander** (keeps things moving).

Three Helpful Tools.

To get the most out of the meeting use three tools: **Check-in** (get meetings off to a good start), **Balcony** (get new perspectives) and **Periscope** (inject a healthy level of continuous improving).

Four Basic Rules.

Keep meetings focused on what matters most by going beyond chit-chat: make concrete proposals (**Propose**), if you don't like a proposal, make a counterproposal (**Counter**), if you do like it, advocate for it (**Advocate**) and when you don't get it, ask (**Enquire**).

In this book I will explain the roles, tools and rules. You'll find more ideas to help you introduce and build the better meeting habits at my website:

www.itsameeting.com.

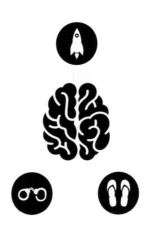

A BETTER MEETING MINDSET.

Unlike my skillset, which predictably and steadily increases over time, my mindset is much more fluid. I can be fully focused in one meeting - leaning in, connecting, supporting and getting things done. Then, in the next meeting, I'm leaning back, distracted, easily annoyed and wasting time. Indeed, I'm back and forth on a continuum all day - between the best version of me, and a version that is much less than my best. No matter where I am on the *mindset continuum*, my skillset doesn't change - at no point do I magically and instantly gain a new skill, then suddenly lose it. But, when I'm the best version of me I do all the things that make meetings work. I propose solutions, ask questions and advocate for others ideas. I keep the meeting, the people and the agenda on track. I nudge, connect and continuously improve. When I'm not the best version of me - usually because I'm stressed, tired, annoyed, overwhelmed or overworked, instead of proposing, enquiring, advocating, nudging, connecting and improving, I become influenced by two sneaky *less than my best* mindsets:

The Tourist Mindset.

When I'm in the Tourist mindset, I'm leaning back and my energy is low. I'm more likely to judge others than support their ideas. Like a Tourist, I've learned enough of the right words to get by, but I'm not fully committed or invested.

The Prisoner Mindset.

When I'm in the Prisoner mindset, I have more energy but it's very negative. Like a prisoner, even though I'm stuck in a prison of my own making, I'm often in denial, blaming and attacking others. I rarely seek to understand or build on ideas. Instead of being productive, I spend time convincing everyone around me to put on handcuffs and be part of the collective prison mindset.

To be clear, I'm not describing a person. Unfortunately, we can't just remove or remediate all the pesky Tourists and Prisoners because they're mindsets, not people. Anyone can get caught in either or both of the Tourist and Prisoner mindsets. It's not possible to be at our best all the time. None of us is perfect. We can slip into the Tourist or Prisoner mindset in an instant. It can last a moment, an hour, a day or even longer. If you don't recognise when the Tourist and Prisoner mindsets are in your meetings, start noticing now. Notice how often and how much time you and colleagues spend in one mindset or the other.

The Better Meeting MindSet.

The simple roles, helpful tools and basic rules help innoculate your meetings against the moments when you and others are not at your best. When you apply the roles, use the tools and commit to the rules regularly you are injecting the meeting with a health-giving, time-saving, energy-boosting vaccine. This better meeting vaccine sharpens your focus - on others and the outcomes of the meeting - and it builds up an immunity to the Tourist and Prisoner mindsets.

Building an immunity.
From crappy to happy meetings.

The best way to build our immunity and improve our meetings is to create new, healthy Better Meeting Habits. All we need do is start a new *habit loop*. Habit loops were codified by Charles Duhigg in his bestselling (highly recommended) book, *The Power of Habit.* The basic idea: your mind is like a computer hard drive. When you want to replace an old program - like an unhelpful habit - you have to write over it with a new updated version. Habit loops are a sort of installation program and the Better Meeting Habits (the roles, tools and rules) are simple apps anyone - with a little patience and persistence - can install.

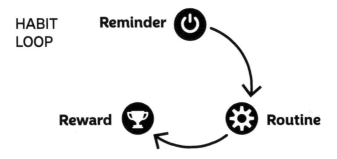

Habit Loops has three steps: the reminder, the routine and the reward. To complete the new habit installation, pay attention to each of the three steps.

⏻ Set-up a Reminder.

To make sure I get through my most important to-do's I type them into a little app on my iPhone. When it's time to get it done a notification pops up to remind me. That's how new habits are started. With notifications and reminders. Luckily, like my to-do app, its quite simple to create better meeting reminders. Afterall, meetings tend to happen in specific rooms and they tend to happen frequently. We could put posters on the wall (*download some here: www.itsameeting.com/posters*) or a note in the notification our calendars send us. The very first action on the written agenda could be appointing a Timekeeper. The second item might be conducting a check-in. It's just a matter of adapting the agenda template. When the Better Meeting Habits are introduced as part of a team effort, the team becomes its own notification system. Sometimes it happens formally, when, for example, a person is given the task of reminding the group to Check-in. Other times, everyone in the group just keeps an informal eye on things and pipes up when the Check-in has been overlooked.

✦ Get into a Routine.

Appointing the Timekeeper is a routine. Keeping the time is another routine. Completing a Check-in at the start of a meeting and using the Periscope at the end are both routines. Having a conversation, being mindful of the four basic rules, also a routine.

The easiest way to get into a routine is to pick a role, a tool or a rule and apply it consistently in as many meeting as you can for a week or two. For example, if you're just starting out with the Better Meeting Habits, you could get into the routine of appointing a Timekeeper at the beginning of a meeting. As each becomes a habit, one after the other, add the Check-in, the Submarine Commander and the Periscope. Finally, when you are ready, get your discussions more focused using the propose and counter rules and be more conscious about your Advocacy and Enquiry. There's absolutely no reason why all these routines couldn't become habits within 6-8 weeks if you apply them frequently and add them to your meetings in small chunks.

When you complete the Better Meeting Assessment (http://survey.itsameeting.com) your personalised report will suggest which routines to start with - based on how you answered the questions and which routines will give you the biggest bang for your buck. Asking your team to complete the assessment will show you which habits to focus on as a group.

Reward new behaviours.

Some might say that better, more productive, effective, and satisfying meetings are a reward in themselves. For example, if you're in the habit of appointing a Timekeeper and managing time effectively, you're going to find your meetings get shorter, you're going to get more done, and you're going to make better decisions and quicker progress. And, you could add a level of extrinsic reward to these intrinsic benefits. Why not, for example, leave the office a little earlier when you notice your meetings are getting shorter.

Building better meeting habits.

Use the roles, tools and rules in this book to over-write your old unhelpful meeting habits. It's your best and quickest route to effective, productive and satisfying meetings.

TIMEKEEPER
AGREE HOW MUCH TIME IS NEEDED, NEGOTIATE EXTENSIONS AND RECOGNISE EXCELLENCE

SUBMARINE COMMANDER
MAKE SURE THE CONVERSATION DOESN'T GO TOO DEEP OR TOO SHALLOW, TOO FAST OR SLOW

Two Simple Roles

80 PERCENT
TIMEKEEPER
IMPROVED MEETINGS

100 PERCENT
SUBMARINE COMMANDER
KEPT MEETINGS FOCUSED

78 PERCENT
MEETINGS BECAME SHORTER

Research conducted in 2016 with large UK bank.

ROLES KEEP YOU FOCUSED

My experience, observing thousands of meetings, suggests that even smart people do dumb things. For example, researchers found: power gets in the way of people working together. In one study, leaders performed less well than junior colleagues because they were too busy competing for status and influence. It's very subtle, but even the most bonded groups lose focus and share less when they come together.

If the science doesn't convince you, sit back and watch it unfold. You will see colleagues get distracted, jockey for position and hold back ideas that they fear might be judged harshly. You might recognise it in yourself. One way to overcome this is to introduce two roles that keep the meeting focused and on track.

START HERE:

Each role has equal importance, but I would introduce the Timekeeper first. It is the simplest to understand, most straightforward to implement and most likely to show immediate results. Ninety-percent of the people who we retested after introducing the better meeting habits said they had used the Timekeeper - eight out of ten said just doing that improved their meetings, and seventy-eight percent reported their meetings became shorter.

All meetings will benefit from the Timekeeper. Try it for a week. If it makes things better, keep doing it. Adding the Submarine Commander (see page 45) will take you quickly to the next level. Any group of people who meet for any meeting can benefit from these roles (from team or project meetings to witches covens).

TIMEKEEPER

Conversation is like gas. It expands to fit the available space. If there are no boundaries, people will talk and talk until the end of the meeting. Deep down we know we shouldn't, but we just can't help ourselves. Even when the meeting has finished, we will keep talking. Some people will stay in the room or on the call. Others will huddle in the corridor. And others will take to eMail or texts to carry on talking.

    Boundaries put a stop to most of that because they reduce the available space and force you to contain the conversation, which is why we use the word *containers*. Effective meetings are broken into containers that hold the conversation and keep you focused.

Chunk your meetings down.

Why do we have meetings? That's a good question. The best answer I know is to *'make decisions and get stuff done'*. Often, after all the talking is done, there's very little space left to achieve either of those. Most of our time is spent discussing the most interesting but least important items and very little time is left to debate the tough but important. Time in meetings can easily get away from us. That's where containers come in. Simply put, containers are: *people in a meeting being deliberate about how much time they spend on what.*

Before you start a conversation agree on the size of the container that is needed to contain the discussion. Some topics – usually the tough but important, need larger containers. Other, less important topics, might need a much smaller container to ensure you don't waste too much time on them. Containers are measured in minutes. In a typical meeting, we should avoid containers that are larger than 60 minutes. Even if you are having a full day meeting on one topic, it is still worth chunking the discussion down into smaller containers.

Who manages the containers?

Someone has to manage those containers. That's the important job of the Timekeeper, who agrees on the size with the group – coaching as necessary if the size feels too large or small. They give gentle reminders if the container is filling quickly, renegotiating when it overflows and recognising when it has been successfully closed. Most of the time, when groups overflow their containers it's because they have either been poorly scoped (they should have been larger) or the conversation isn't being managed. Both of those issues are easily solved with good time management and a watchful Submarine Commander (see page 45).

Timekeepers are not the police.

You might imagine the Timekeeper is a policing role. When groups have that mindset, they usually assign the role to the groups grumpiest member. I would counsel against this. Share the role around so everyone participates actively in creating the norms that will make your meetings better. And remember, managing time is a positive thing that focuses the team. Make sure the Timekeeper is seen as a positive influencer, not an annoying policeman who is there to get in the way of a necessary discussion or debate.

And avoid becoming a slave to the clock. Flex the container size to ensure the best decisions are being made, while keeping the group present to the agreements it made. There's a delicate balance here that is more subtle than most people think.

When a decision is made, close the container. When the container is closed, move on. If a decision must be deferred because it needs more time or input, agree on a next step and close the container.

What does it look like?

At the start of the meeting quickly agree who will take on the role of the Timekeeper. Of course, they can use their watch or smartphone, but I recommend a visual timer. My favourite is the 12" TimeTimer, which visually communicates elapsed time and beeps when the container is full. Everyone can see it happening in front of them. Hopefully, the group has an agenda or a structure for the meeting. For each important topic, the Timekeeper quickly agrees the size (in mins) of each container. It's tempting to divvy up the time equally between topics, but this might not be the best approach. Focus on the priorities first. Make sure you're giving the important stuff the time it needs to move it forward.

The start of the meeting is the right place to spend a few minutes on timekeeping so you waste less time later. When you have agreed on the size of your containers, the Timekeeper nudges the group when appropriate. Being the Timekeeper shouldn't limit your role. You're still a member of the team, so keep participating fully. It is not a pass to step out of your responsibilities as a participant and team member.

If it's important to continue the conversation but the container is closing, negotiate with the group to extend the container. Avoid ignoring the container by continuing without recognising and adjusting. That is the path to the dark side. If you lose the discipline, it will slip away and you will be back to endless chit-chat.

Finally, if you are keeping time, recognise the moments of excellence, when the group makes decisions before the container has closed.

Summary:
The **Timekeeper**:
- Negotiates the size (in minutes) of each container;
- Keeps a watchful eye on the time and nudges when appropriate;
- Negotiates extensions to the container size if needed;
- Recognises excellence as it happens.

SUBMARINE COMMANDER

Who is driving this meeting? That's a question I often ask when I'm observing a group. Most of the time it feels like no one is at the helm. The meeting drifts along at its own pace and in its own good time. If it's a team meeting then maybe the boss is leading it, because that's what bosses do? It's their job to boss everyone around. I find that quite amusing. When I see the boss start to take charge, it's usually after I have had a long conversation with them about their on-going disappointment with the team's inability to take the initiative. The boss will tell me how frustrated he is that they don't step up. When I talk to the team, they say: 'he doesn't let us'. I don't think either of them is being tricky or that they intend to mess with each other's heads. A dynamic starts to build up between the leader and the followers. She leads. They follow. Like a tango. Someone has to lead, and someone has to follow. It's a dynamic. It happens too when meetings have a chairperson. The chair leads. Everyone else follows. The chair, in effect, becomes the defacto boss. Lead. Follow. It's a dynamic.

Unfortunately, breaking the dynamic isn't as easy as telling the boss/chair to step back and the team to step up. That rarely sticks. What you have to do is create a new, more effective dynamic to replace the old one. The easiest way to do that is to create informal *leadership* roles within the meeting that everyone can have a go at... like the Timekeeper and Submarine Commander.

Focus on depth and propulsion.

We don't want just to make another bossy boss. The idea is to create a sense of shared ownership and equality in the meeting, not just share the bossy role. So, in addition to the Timekeeper we have a second role called the Submarine Commander (or Subcomm) - who keeps things focused and moving. The Submarine Commander is there to make sure the submarine (aka conversation) doesn't go too deep or too shallow, too fast or too slow. In other words, they are there to monitor depth and propulsion.

THE DEADLY SHALLOWS

THE BOTTOM OF THE DEEP BLUE SEA

THREE REASONS YOU NEED A SUBMARINE COMMANDER:

1. Keep the Submarine from going to the bottom of the deep blue sea.

Often in a meeting the conversation goes way too deep. People get on a roll and start enthusiastically sharing the technical specifications of the new X101 widget or getting into the nitty-gritty of the latest marketing plan or people strategy. Unless this is a room full of X101 engineers or the marketing teams planning session, this is not the meeting to be talking about either of those things. If you go too deep, you will use all your oxygen on things that are not important and the meeting will be all *talk, no action*.

2. Keep the Submarine out of the deadly shallows.

Sometimes meetings get a bit fluffy, and you don't talk about the important stuff. This might be because there is tension or conflict that attendees don't want to confront. It could be that no one knows what is important. Quite a lot of the time it is because smaller groups of people have already had the conversation, in an offline meeting, and no one wants to open a can of worms, where the outcome might be different from the previously hatched plan. Whatever the reason, if you are going to stay in the shallows you're wasting your time. Either agree not to have the meeting at all or take the conversation a bit deeper and have that uncomfortable conversation you have been avoiding.

3. Keep the meetings from going off course.

It's not uncommon for conversations to go off on a tangent. It will usually be two or three people who start talking about something that genuinely interests them, but is not relevant to anyone else. They probably don't even realise they are doing it but very quickly the submarine is way off course and the people not involved in this sidebar conversation are too busy checking their iPhones to notice. Time itself may be infinite but the time you have with your colleagues to talk about important business topics is not. While diversions *might* allow for spontaneity of thought and *may* be useful if that's what is needed (and sometimes it is needed), they will slow you down and switch people off.

Introduce an active observer.

The Submarine Commander is what I call an active observer, less involved in the conversation than everyone else because they are focused more on the process than the content. People have for too long been allowed to let the submarine bounce around from the deadly shallows to the bottom of the deep blue sea. They are experts at taking the submarine off course to their own little island where they've hidden their personal agendas and interests. The Submarine Commander is there to gently nudge the submarine back on course when that happens because the conversation is too important to leave to chance. And your job, Submarine Commander, is more important than your contribution to the conversation, so pay attention.

The Submarine Commander is not the boss of everyone but they are the one person in the room who is fully focused on the meeting and the outcomes and the value being created, so they're worth paying attention to. Give the Submarine Commander some respect. The role can change between meetings. And it can change in the meeting. So it might be you who next has the awesome responsibility of getting the group where they need to be (even if they don't necessarily want to get there in a hurry).

What does it look like?

At the beginning of the meeting, after you have agreed who will take the Timekeeper role, appoint a Submarine Commander. You could do it before the meeting, particularly if you have an agenda. Share the role around a bit so everyone gets a go. If one or two people are outstanding Submarine Commanders then why not use them more, but they might also be better used to coach others who might be doing that thing we do to get out of the household chores – you know, pretending we are not very good at them. It's a pretty cool role, and it doesn't exclude you from contributing, but you should keep the conversation and meeting on course first and foremost.

When the Subcomm is appointed, it's a good practice for them to set-up the Check-in (see page 61) and use the Periscope (see page 87) to help the group continuously improve. They're usually pretty good at knowing when to go on the Balcony (see page 77).

Better Meeting Assessment.

As far as the simple roles go, in meetings that are effective:

- People are almost always clear exactly how much time they have to discuss topics before they start talking;

- When discussions go off track someone almost always immediately calls it and they get back on track quickly.

If you haven't already used the Better Meeting Assessment to see how useful the two simple roles might be, you can complete it on your smartphone, tablet, PC or Mac here:

http://survey.itsameeting.com

CHECK-IN
TAKE-OFF BY CONNECTING
AT A HUMAN LEVEL

BALCONY
ZOOM OUT AND
NOTICE WHAT IS GOING ON

PERISCOPE
ADD A HEALTHY DOSE OF
CONTINUOUS IMPROVEMENT

It's a Meeting not Rocket Science

Three Helpful Tools

PERCENT
TRIED ONE OR MORE TOOL AND
QUALITY OF MEETINGS IMPROVED

PERCENT
USED THE CHECK-IN SAID
MEETINGS BECAME SHORTER

PERCENT
MEETING SATISFACTION
IMPROVEMENT IN 4 WEEKS

Research conducted in 2016 with large UK bank.

TOOLS MAKE LIFE EASIER

Tools have been used for millennium to make work easier. The first cave dwellers made basic tools to make life that little bit easier. Craftsmen use tools to improve the quality of their work and to complete tasks efficiently with minimal time. And professionals use tools because they are a sure way of increasing accuracy and minimising waste. With that in mind, here are three simple, practical tools that will help the group be at their best.

When we use these tools, it will make the job easier, faster and more accurate. Each tool has been tested and is proven to add value. They are all worth the time to learn and use and will all pay back dividends when you waste less time later.

START HERE:

Like the Timekeeper, the Check-in is simple, easy and a quick win. Our research shows, the simple practice of *checking-in* with ourselves and others at the start of a meeting creates more openness, promotes deeper listening, builds more connections and helps us better understand each other over time – all factors that improve meetings. Start your meetings with a Check-in for the next week. If it works, keep doing it.

Then, introduce the Periscope at the end of meetings to lock in what is working and agree how to make the next meeting even better. You'll also want to start using the Balcony - an easy way to zoom out, get new perspectives, break tension, shake up auto-pilot discussions and generate new insight.

CHECK-IN

Do you get stressed? Annoyed? Overwhelmed? Are you ever distracted? Do you bring any of that into your work and meetings? Imagine being a pilot or a surgeon and think about what happens if you are stressed, overwhelmed and exhausted on the job. Consider the impact of being distracted by simmering, unresolved emotions or unspoken interpersonal frustrations. The consequences would not be good. Decisions would be impaired; miscommunications become commonplace; relationships get stretched to breaking-point and basic, rookie mistakes made. We all suffer, at times, from poor decision making and breakdowns in communication and connection with others. And we all make mistakes when we are tired and frustrated and stressed and overwhelmed. For us, it might not have life or death consequences, but it still impacts the quality of our work, our relationships, our listening and our decision making.

Often it's the *stuff* we bring in from home, the journey in, or previous meetings. That unresolved argument we had with our spouse. The traffic that painfully edged along and caused us to miss our morning Latte. It's even worse when we are running from meeting to meeting all day. We might end up at a late afternoon meeting with *stuff* from all the meetings we've attended through the day. Plus, now we are thinking about the traffic home and the uncomfortable conversations waiting for us when you get there. Most of the time our stresses, annoyances and frustrations sit inside of us. They bubble and spit and hiss inside like volcanic sludge. It eats away at our focus. We emotionally and intellectually drift in and out of the meeting.

The *stuff* I'm talking about is partly thoughts, all the things we should have done, could have said and would have raised if only we had been a little more present. And it is partly feelings: the sharp cut of anger from the 9 am conference call with a blameful client. The frustration sparked from another wasted hour at the 11 am committee meeting. Sadness from 1 pm's farewell speech. This is precisely why a simple process called the Check-in has become a habit for pilots, surgeon and many other professions.

The difference Check-ins make.

Helicoptor pilots ferrying people to and from oil-rigs were one of the first groups to start using a version of the Check-in. Helicopters were ditching in the ocean without mechanical issues at fault. Human error was a disproportionately large cause of the accidents. Investigators found tension in the cockpit, distractions and miscommunication all played a role, causing poor decisions and stupid mistakes. After pilots started checking-in before each flight incidents decreased. When commercial airline crash investigators looked into unexplained accidents, they noticed co-pilots held back critical information from the pilot because they feared a negative reaction, so entrenched was the 'pilot is god' culture in the cockpit. Now, flight crews perform a technical check and a human check-in to ensure everyone feels comfortable speaking up. A large bank I worked with found colleagues were afraid to escalate concerns to leaders, which led to billion dollar fines and, according to Homeland

Security, thousands of deaths relating to money laundering. They added the Check-in as part of a suite of measures to break down hierarchy and bring back humility. When operating, surgical teams also Check-in to break down the hierarchy and quickly connect.

Today, before pilots fly and surgeons operate, and before enlightened business professionals meet, there is a moment of human connection, a putting aside of distractions and a getting on the same page around task and intention. That is what a Check-in does.

What does it look like?

For the first few minutes, each participant answers two question (plus an optional question if time allows) to connect, exorcise unresolved distractions and get their head in the game. There are no wrong answers and it is not a dialogue, so it helps if everyone suspends judgement and listens. When each person has spoken, we say thanks. And if someone doesn't want to check-in, they do not have to.

There are many questions that might be helpful, but two are proven to make a difference quickly:

Q1. How am I feeling?

Just one word. A brief explanation if it feels right. For example:

> 'I feel happy to be here and grateful to be involved' or

> 'I'm frustrated because I don't think we are making enough progress'.

When the Check-in is complete, and we have heard how each person is feeling, we can respond more considerately to colleagues' circumstances and needs, which builds trust and deepens our connection. If we know Bob has landed in the room frustrated about his budget cuts we can adapt accordingly. If Ed tells us he's exhausted because he's been up all night with a sick child we can take that into consideration. And if Jane is stressed, totally snowed under preparing an urgent report for the board, maybe we can cut her some slack. It doesn't mean we have to cater to every need or talk endlessly about every feeling everyone has in every moment. We share what's important and use the knowledge to progress the meeting in the most effective way. Irritating Bob or pressuring Jane is most likely going to make things worse, not better.

Getting my feeling on the table at the top of the meeting also gives me a good indicator of any personal triggers that might get in the way of being at my best. If I declare my frustration with the progress of the project, recognising I am triggered might help me as much as it helps others. Often, just getting it out there makes me feel better, but I can also own my trigger and do something about it - like, taking a deep breath or giving myself a good talking to. If I learn others also feel frustrated, this could be a good discussion point, after the Check-in but before we dive into the prepared agenda. We can talk about what is slowing us down? I could also learn that I'm the only one concerned about the speed of progress. Good to know. Maybe I need to chill-down!

When it's all 'good'.

One thing you might notice is people robotically using the word 'good', which is more of an assessment of our feelings and not an emotion. That's fine. Whatever. From time to time, it won't hurt to remind people there are lots of words that describe emotions, like: angry, bored, anxious, excited, frustrated, suspicious, relieved, impatient, disappointed, grateful, worried, happy, irritated, overwhelmed, surprised, hopeful, shocked, vulnerable, calm, confident, curious, positive, stressed and tired. I've personally been all of those in a meeting at some point. If groups struggle to connect fully with their feelings, I've suggested people draw emoji faces or choose a photo of a person expressing an emotion.

We don't have to make this a big deal, but the more precise we are and the more honest we are about how we really feel, the more helpful the declaration will be (to us and others).

Q2. What could prevent me from being fully present?

It's possible nothing is distracting you and you are fully present. Great. It's equally likely you have eMails that have not been replied to, reports unfinished, calls or meetings with colleagues or customers to prepare for and unresolved issues waiting to be dealt with when the meeting ends. Just saying the words can, bizarrely, help to quiet the distractions and give you back the bandwidth you'll need for a more focused meeting. And, if the rest of the room is aware of the things that are eating at you, maybe they can help. In a recent meeting I attended, a colleague shared with the team his wife had been taken to hospital overnight and that might prevent him from being fully present. The meeting was immediately stopped and rescheduled. Although it was essential for the colleague to be at the meeting at some point, everyone in the room agreed it was more important for their colleague to be with his wife. It was an easy decision to postpone the meeting. That doesn't happen every day. But most meetings are longer than they need to be. If we know people in the room have other pressing matters to deal with, we could agree to power through and finish sooner. We could switch agenda items to allow someone to step out early instead of making them waste forty-five minutes waiting for their turn to speak, particularly if we know they have something urgent to deliver. No matter our role title, our most important job is to be a human being. This question helps us do that.

The Third Question.

The option is there for a third, more meeting or business need specific question. It is not essential to ask this, but I find, more often than not, it's useful - particularly if the meeting is longer. Unlike questions one (feelings) and two (distractions), which I recommend you use consistently, the third question is not fixed. That said, not all questions are made equal, so I have some suggestions:

- What is my intention?
- What is keeping me awake at night?
- How will I show up today?
- What do I want to create in this meeting?
- What am I grateful for?
- What do I love about..?
- What do I need to let go of?
- What concerns or doubts do I have?
- How will I create value for our customers?
- What will I contribute today?

These are just examples. They all work but may or may not be right for a specific moment. Everyone answers the same question and anyone can offer a suggestion.

Merely discussing the third question can contribute to team bonding and a better meeting. I work with the board of a European bank. One of the highlights of their meetings is agreeing on the third question, in which everyone, including the industry veteran chief executive, enthusiastically participates. There's lots of laughter, followed by a deep level of honesty, which is not a bad way to start a meeting. The CEO directly attributes an increase in team effectiveness, decision making and improved outcomes, to the Check-in and the third question. It really can be worth the small investment in time.

Who goes first?

The most efficient way of moving around the group is to ask someone to start, then the person to their left (or right) goes until everyone is done. Some teams prefer popcorn style, where people pop when they're ready. It's a more random, slower process but sometimes speed isn't the point – especially if there are underlying issues in the group. Everyone should feel they could go first if that's what they want. Whatever feels right at that moment is probably right. Whoever goes first models the process and sets the tone, depth and speed for everyone else.

Is it worth the time?

You might be wondering if, after you have all checked-in, there will be any time left to have the meeting. Now, I know this is counter-intuitive, but over seventy-eight percent of people that often or almost always start their meetings with a moment to check-in and get fully present, tell us one benefit has been shorter meetings. Yes, you read that correctly. Even when they spent time on something that wasn't directly related to the meeting topic, the meeting ended sooner. To be clear, that might not happen the first, second or third time you Check-in. This tool has a longer burn than the Timekeeper or Periscope, which can have an immediate impact. It takes time to build trust, to connect at a deeper, more human level and for the focus muscle to grow. But over time, after a week or two, the few minutes you invest in checking-in will give you a healthy return on your investment. It's just two to three simple questions and a moment of bearing, sharing or caring from each person in the room. Give it a go. What do you have to lose?

BALCONY

Have you ever been in a meeting and, sooner or later, realised you have no idea what is going on? If you're anything like me, you probably kept a low profile until the end of the meeting and tackled a colleague in the corridor to ask, "what the frick was that about?"

What about meetings where everyone is on auto-pilot or just going through the motions? And then there are those meetings that feel tense or negative or, worse, full of unresolved conflicts that everyone is desperate to ignore. Have you ever been in one of those meetings? Have you been in a meeting where you, the team, or the conversation just got stuck?

If you answered yes to just one of these questions, and I suspect you've been in all those meetings at some point and more than once, the Balcony is the perfect tool for you. It isn't the same as the Check-in, which has a set time and place in the meeting, so it takes a bit of self and group awareness - which is where having an active observer, like the Submarine Commander, comes in handy. Someone needs to notice the group is stuck, in conflict, on auto-pilot or not making any sense. Someone has to call it and encourage the group to step on the Balcony. Then, when the stuck becomes unstuck and the tension is released, and sense is being made, and the auto-pilot has been disengaged, someone has to take the group back off the Balcony so fresh perspectives and insights can be taken advantage of. The perfect job for a Submarine Commander but also something anyone in the meeting can make happen.

What is the Balcony?

Just to be clear, the Balcony is metaphorical. You don't need to leave the meeting physically. The Balcony is a place to zoom out as a group and make a conscious effort to notice what is going on. Let's say, for example, it is becoming obvious there are elephants in the room that are getting in the way of progress and no one is talking about them. Great, now we can step up on the Balcony, notice what is happening and get some fresh perspectives. Then, we step off the balcony, bringing new insights to the meeting. It's important we step on *and* off because staying in a constant state of zoomed-out will lead to confusion and paralysis. It's like using Google Maps. You zoom out to see the wider terrain:

the network of roads, off-ramps, villages, roadworks and jams. Then you come down to earth to see the immediate twists and turns and take action in the real world using what you learned from your high-level helicopter view. If you stayed at ten-thousand feet, you would not know when and where to make the turns that will get you home.

The word *Balcony* comes from Ronald A. Heifetz, a professor at the Havard Business School. His analogy takes us into a nightclub, which has a dance floor and a balcony overlooking the dancers. When we are in a meeting, avoiding the elephants in the room, we are in the dance of work. We see the people closest to us on the dance floor, moving to the music. We can see how each of them is behaving close up, what they are doing, what they are wearing and what is right in front of us. When we stop dancing and step up on the balcony, our view widens. Now we see the group dynamic more clearly (how everyone is moving together or moving differently). We see trends and patterns that were not visible when we were in the dance. Away from the dance we also start to notice the elephants and hidden agendas and assumptions and undercurrents. We see some people are not dancing in the same way as other, almost as if more than one song is playing. Some people are not dancing at all. When we have seen the wider picture and noticed the things we had not seen from our position on the dance floor, new thoughts and perspectives might be clearer to us. We may get a better sense of the priorities and the possibilities. If we stayed on the balcony, those new insights would have little value. Now, we need to get back to the dance floor, our dance of work, to gain value from the insights, to synchronise our dancing or at least bring it closer together. For each step up on the Balcony, we take a step back to the dance floor.

I do not often dance in nightclubs, but I do recognise the dance of work. I get that sometimes it would be useful to see the dance floor from the balcony and to bring any insights I get from that perceptual position back to my dancing, particularly if everyone on the dance floor has the same new insights. So, in that sense, the analogy works and the name, *balcony*, makes sense. We go up on the Balcony when the group is stuck, going through the motions, in conflict, avoiding, unproductive or going around in circles. When fresh perspectives, priorities or possibilities have emerged, we step off the Balcony and get back to the dance of work.

We can use our Balcony time in a number of ways. And going on an even higher balcony might reveal new ways to get more benefits from this simple, powerful tool. For now, groups I've worked with have found three questions to be useful. I offer them here as a jumping in point. Feel free to experiment, adapt and improve.

Go on the balcony and discuss:

1. What is happening?
Notice the group dynamics, the trends, patterns, language and behaviours.

2. What are we not seeing?
Notice the elephants in the room, hidden agendas and assumptions, and hear from the quieter voices.

3. What now becomes possible?
Notice any emerging perspectives, possibilities and priorities.

What does it look like?

A meeting I attended recently was going nowhere fast. Some of the group were engaged in a deep conversation that did not seem to interest others, and there were clearly issues that no one wanted to talk about. One of the participants, who was leaning back quietly observing, later described it as 'cats circling the porridge'. I had offered to be Submarine Commander, so I stopped the meeting and asked the group to join me on the Balcony. I could have waited and used the Periscope to bring my observations into the room, but that would not have helped the group at this critical moment. It took a little courage, but I was sure it was the right thing to do. I started by asking the group what they noticed about the behaviours in the room. They talked about the lack of participation from some and the over-participation of others. We discussed the Check-in, which felt negative and tense. When I asked what we were not seeing, someone bravely put the spotlight on the elephant. She shared her assumptions about it and how not dealing with it was impacting her. Others agreed. Some added different perspectives. The group invited the quieter voices to chip in and were surprised by their thoughtful, reflective comments. When we got to the third question, what now becomes possible, ideas began to flow and the group quickly reached consensus on a new way forward. When we stepped off the Balcony, the meeting progressed quickly and ended with a lot of positive energy.

From start to finish I do not think our Balcony conversation took more than fifteen minutes. I'm certain, in the long run, it has saved hours of wasted time and energy.

PERISCOPE

Lately, professional cycling has not been the best role model. Even so, I'm going to use the example of Team Sky here because I genuinely believe their philosophy of Marginal Gains made a difference, even if it wasn't the only thing that did. Team Sky was born in 2009 with the ambitious - some said impossible - goal of a British rider winning the Tour de France within five years. In 2017, just eight years later, they collected their fifth win. An extraordinary achievement, which they largely attributed to what they call, Marginal Gains - **the small things that make a big difference**.

For example, in competition, they swapped out dirty and lumpy hotel mattresses for the riders specially made, hyper-clean bedding. The slightly better sleep on a familiar mattress led to slightly faster race times. Small changes to diet, exercise, start times, etc also made marginal gains to wellbeing, fitness levels and ability to compete. These and thousands of other small things made a big difference. Team Sky obsessively look for, test and build on these small changes, injecting a healthy and winning dose of continuous improvement in everything they do. We can use Marginal Gains to continuously improve our meetings. Luckily we don't need a team of coaches, medics, dieticians and psychologists like Team Sky. We just need the Periscope - our third helpful tool - and two simple questions. I called this tool the Periscope because it's a device on a submarine that widens our viewpoint and brings greater clarity. The submarine analogy might suggest it's a tool for the Submarine Commander, which is partly true, but in our world, everyone is encouraged to use the Periscope (for meetings and beyond).

What does it look like?

At the end of a meeting a few minutes are allocated to answering two simple questions:

Q1. What worked well?
Q2. What could we do to make our next meeting even better?

Q1. What worked well?

A moment to recognise what we did in the meeting that moved us forward, helped us make better decisions or build connections or get the best out of each other. When we become aware of our positive actions, we are more likely to lock them in and keep doing them. It also makes us feel good.

Q2. What could we do to make our next meeting even better?

There is always more we can do to improve our meetings. Every meeting has a Marginal Gain for us to find and act on. You'll notice I'm not suggesting you talk about what isn't working or what you didn't do. When you only have a few minutes, it's much more productive and rewarding to spend the time looking for one or two constructive ideas, experiments or commitments, rather than kicking around our failings and mistakes.

The active observer.

Because the Submarine Commander is on the edge of the meeting she can share what she noticed from her active observer perspective. That's an excellent place to start. If she has to share observations at the end of the meeting, she might also stay focused and pay attention in the meeting. It also makes sense to have a quick brainstorm where anyone who has a view shares it.

Make it snappy.

Time will dictate how wide and how deep you go with the Periscope. The basic principle is continuous improvement - the smallest things can make the biggest difference. How often you use the Periscope matters more than how long you spend using it. Each time you use it, there is an opportunity for the group to improve. It only takes a moment, and it's so simple and easy. Why wouldn't you use it at least a couple of times a week?

Choose to, not have to.

To be clear, the Check-in, Balcony and Periscope are helpful tools, not mandatory processes. It is not essential that every meeting has any or all of them. I don't check-in to every meeting, and I only go on the Balcony when it's needed. Some meetings wouldn't benefit from the Periscope. If the tools become rote or a tick-the-box exercise, they lose some of their magic. And, that said, when you use them they make meetings better. The evidence also suggests, when you use them more your meetings become better, faster. The key, I think, is to try them out with an open mind. If they create value for you and the people you meet with, it's an easy choice to keep using them. But it is much better when you *choose*, and don't *have* to use them.

Better Meeting Assessment.

As far as the helpful tools go, in meetings that are effective:

- People almost always take a moment to check-in and get fully present at the start;

- At the end of meetings people often take time to evaluate performance and agree how we could improve in the future.

If you haven't already used the Better Meeting Assessment to see how useful the helpful tools might be, you can complete it on your smartphone, tablet, PC or Mac here:

http://survey.itsameeting.com

PROPOSE
SOMEONE MAKES A PROPOSAL.
JUST SAY: 'I PROPOSE WE...'
AND A DISCUSSION ENSUES

COUNTER
IF YOU DON'T LIKE IT, MAKE A
COUNTER-PROPOSAL.
YOU CAN'T JUST THROW A
SPANNER IN AND WALK AWAY

ADVOCATE
IF YOU LIKE A PROPOSAL
ADVOCATE FOR IT.
OFFER EVIDENCE & EXPERTISE
TO HELP BUILD A CASE

ENQUIRE
IF YOU DON'T GET IT,
ASK QUESTIONS.
QUESTIONS CREATE DIALOGUE
AND ENCOURAGE DEBATE

It's a Meeting not Rocket Science

Four Basic Rules

A BETTER SET OF BASIC RULES

Life has rules (thou shalt not steal). Sport has rules (first past the post). And work has an ever-growing, seemingly endless list of rules. If we so willingly accept (and mostly appreciate) the rules in life, sport and work, why does having rules in a meeting make some people a bit uncomfortable? It doesn't make much sense because, even when we don't have explicitly agreed rules that help, we almost always have unwritten ones that don't. For example, there's the *Roulette Rule*. Roulette is a game of chance in which a ball bounces around and - hopefully - lands on a number that favours us. In meetings, the *Roulette Rule* allows 'players' to bounce ideas around the wheel of fortune, hoping, before the meeting ends, the ball lands on an idea that works.

Then we have the *Spanner Rule*, which allows any player to throw a spanner in the works - finding problems with other people's ideas, without any responsibility for offering alternative solutions.

The third unwritten rule of meetings is the *Sink/Swim Rule*, in which all players - no matter the merit of their ideas, are left to sink or swim by colleagues who choose not to speak in support of others.

The fourth unwritten rule is the *Revolving Door Rule*. If players don't understand a proposal, they dismiss it and move on to the next.

No one goes into a meeting and announces an intention to follow these unwritten rules. They won't appear on an intranet page or shiny poster on the wall. But they do exist and are present in millions of meetings, every day, all over the world. All I am suggesting is a better set of basic rules that improve the game and make it more satisfying for players.

What does it look like?

- Ditch the *Roulette Rule* and leave nothing to chance. Instead, make clear proposals that can be discussed and debated.

- If we don't like a proposal, let's agree to throw out the *Spanner Rule* and throw in alternative solutions and counterproposals.

- We say no to the *Sink/Swim Rule* and decide to get behind other peoples ideas - with our support and expertise - when we dig it.

- When we don't understand something we ignore the *Revolving Door Rule* and ask a question instead.

That's the four basic rules. We agree to propose, counter, advocate and enquire.

PROPOSE
(Ditch the Roulette Rule)
SOMEONE HAS TO MAKE A PROPOSAL
JUST SAY: 'I PROPOSE WE...'

You can't just keep bouncing from one idea to the next. Someone has to put forward a definite proposal that can be discussed and debated. It might not be what gets agreed, but it's a start. Popcorn thinking, where teams quickly bounce from one unresolved idea to the next, is one of the hardest habits you will need to break, but break it you must. At some point, and the earlier the better, someone has to make a proposal. They say, 'I propose we...' and a discussion ensues.

COUNTER
(Throw out the Spanner Rule)
IF YOU DON'T LIKE A PROPOSAL MAKE A COUNTER-PROPOSAL.

If you don't like the proposal, you can't just throw a spanner in the works and walk away. You don't have time for that. Instead, make a counterproposal. Then the team can debate the merits of one proposal over the other. And you can't just add the words 'I counter that…' on the front of a stream of new ideas. Slow down and discuss the ideas that have been proposed. Slow is smooth. Smooth is fast. Spend the time debating real proposals, not brainstorming lots of ideas.

ADVOCATE
(Say no to the Sink/Swim Rule)
IF YOU LIKE A PROPOSAL, ADVOCATE FOR IT
OFFER EVIDENCE AND EXPERTISE.

If you like the proposal, advocate for it. You are there as part of a group. If a colleagues' idea has merit, then speak up in support of it. Offer evidence and use your expertise to help them build their case. And if your proposal has been countered, you don't have to just go along with the new idea. If your proposal is worth it, fight for it (not literally!), strengthen it and encourage others to build on it. The key here is to speak with purpose, not just because you like the sound of your voice.

ENQUIRE
(Ignore the Revolving Door Rule)
IF YOU DON'T GET IT, ASK QUESTIONS
QUESTIONS CREATE DIALOGUE.

I'm always surprised how few questions people ask. Where did our curiosity go? When we were children, we asked an endless stream of questions. What happened? When people ask questions, a real conversation emerges. Ideas solidify and grow. People get animated and involved. We're bored of the monologuing. It switches us off. Questions create a dialogue. And they switch us back on. If you don't get it or doubt something will work, ask a question to clarify and confirm.

RULES ARE MADE TO BE BROKEN

Even when rules aren't made that way, we can usually find an exception where breaking the rule makes sense. That is also true of the four basic rules. They can and should be broken from time to time. I don't want to suck the life out of your meetings and leave them feeling too rigid or lacking spontaneity. If you have a brainstorm, nobody has to make a proposal. If you are spitballing ideas, it might not be essential to stop the flow of energy for a tough question. I get that. And, the purpose of most meetings is not brainstorming and spitballing. The purpose is to *make decisions and get stuff done*. If that's your objective, you will find these basic rules very helpful - most of the time. Try using them for a week. If they work, keep using them.

It's a Meeting not Rocket Science

The whole thing on eight pages

ONE MANUAL FOR EVERY MEETING

My goal with this little book was to put in your hands a manual for better, more productive, effective and satisfying meetings. By combining the simple, easy to use and proven ideas in this book with the Better Meeting Assessment, that gives you a personalised report with specific actions, I know you can immediately make a difference to your meetings. If you have not already completed the Better Meeting Assessment it will take you less than three minutes on your desktop, smartphone or tablet:

http://survey.itsameeting.com

Let me know if you make progress or get stuck. Your input helps make this book better. Contact me via email here:

jason@itsameeting.com

TWO SIMPLE ROLES

TIMEKEEPER
AGREE HOW MUCH TIME IS NEEDED, NEGOTIATE EXTENSIONS AND RECOGNISE EXCELLENCE

SUBMARINE COMMANDER
MAKE SURE THE CONVERSATION DOESN'T GO TOO DEEP OR TOO SHALLOW, TOO FAST OR SLOW

www.itsameeting.com

THREE HELPFUL TOOLS

CHECK-IN
TAKE-OFF BY CONNECTING
AT A HUMAN LEVEL

BALCONY
ZOOM OUT AND
NOTICE WHAT IS GOING ON

PERISCOPE
ADD A HEALTHY DOSE OF
CONTINUOUS IMPROVEMENT

www.itsameeting.com

FOUR BASIC RULES

PROPOSE
SOMEONE MAKES A PROPOSAL.
JUST SAY: 'I PROPOSE WE...'
AND A DISCUSSION ENSUES

COUNTER
IF YOU DON'T LIKE IT, MAKE A COUNTER-PROPOSAL.
YOU CAN'T JUST THROW A
SPANNER IN AND WALK AWAY

ADVOCATE
IF YOU LIKE A PROPOSAL ADVOCATE FOR IT.
OFFER EVIDENCE & EXPERTISE
TO HELP BUILD A CASE

ENQUIRE
IF YOU DON'T GET IT, ASK QUESTIONS.
QUESTIONS CREATE DIALOGUE
AND ENCOURAGE DEBATE

www.itsameeting.com

CHECK-IN
CONNECT AT A HUMAN LEVEL FIRST

Q1. How am I feeling?

Just one word. A brief explanation if it feels right. For example:

- *'I feel happy to be here and grateful to be involved' or*
- *'I'm frustrated because I don't think we are making enough progress'.*

Q2. What could prevent me from being fully present?

- *Not yet replied to eMails,*
- *Unfinished reports,*
- *Calls or meetings with colleagues or customers to prepare for and*
- *Unresolved issues waiting to be dealt with after the meeting.*

www.itsameeting.com

The Third Question.

An optional third, more meeting or business need specific question. For example:
- *What is my intention for the meeting?*
- *What is keeping me awake at night?*
- *How will I show up today?*
- *What do I want to create in this meeting?*
- *What am I grateful for?*
- *What do I love about..?*
- *What do I need to let go of?*
- *What concerns or doubts do I have?*
- *How will I create value for our customers?*
- *What will I contribute today?*

www.itsameeting.com

BALCONY
ZOOM OUT & NOTICE WHAT IS GOING ON

Go on the balcony and discuss:

1. What is happening?

- *Notice the group dynamics, the trends, patterns, language and behaviours.*

2. What are we not seeing?

- *Notice the elephants in the room, hidden agendas and assumptions, and hear from the quieter voices.*

3. What now becomes possible?

- *Notice any emerging perspectives, possibilities and priorities.*

www.itsameeting.com

PERISCOPE
ADD CONTINUOUS IMPROVEMENT

At the end of the meeting a few minutes are allocated to answering two simple questions:

Q1. What worked well?

- *Recognise what moved us forward, helped us make better decisions or got the best out of each other.*

Q2. What could we do to make our next meeting even better?

- *When you only have a few minutes we spend the time looking for ideas, experiments and commitments.*

www.itsameeting.com

timekeeper	subcomm	check-in	balcony	periscope

www.itsameeting.com

timekeeper	subcomm	check-in	balcony	periscope

www.itsameeting.com

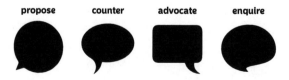

www.itsameeting.com

timekeeper   **subcomm**   **check-in**   **balcony**   **periscope**

www.itsameeting.com

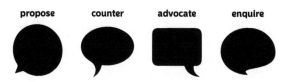

www.itsameeting.com

timekeeper subcomm check-in balcony periscope

www.itsameeting.com

ABOUT THE AUTHOR

Author | Facilitator | Designer |
I make work better by designing and facilitating cultural and human change.

Jason is the founder of **AT OUR BEST** and **AT OUR BEST** LAB - consulting and creative design agencies for culture, leadership and organisational transformation. He partners with organisations to shape culture, improve teams and help people be at their best.

Jason works with organisations across Europe, Asia, Latin and North America, South Africa, India and Australia.

Connect with Jason:
www.itsameeting.com
jason@itsameeting.com
instagram.com/_jasonmoore

APPRECIATION

There is no doubt I would not have been able to write this book without the endless support of my wife, Erika. I have been blessed with someone who selflessly contributes ideas, suggestions and expertise. She deserves more credit than she gets.

I'd also like to acknowledge the long list of clients, mentors, colleagues and friends that I get to play and grow with. So many committed human beings who care about making work and life better.

That I get to work with these awesome people is nothing short of a miracle.

Thank you all.

IT'S A MEETING
NOT ROCKET SCIENCE
a manual for meetings ─────────

PUBLISHED BY
AT OUR BEST LTD

ISBN: 978-1-9996180-0-1

© Jason Moore 2016 & 2018.
All Rights Reserved.

Made in the USA
San Bernardino, CA
31 December 2018